Daring Devotion

Compiled by
Lisa-Marie Pusch

Release International

Release helps Christians in the UK and Ireland to actively engage with their persecuted brothers and sisters around the world: praying for them, standing with them, helping them, and learning lessons of true Christian discipleship with them.

Romanian pastor Richard Wurmbrand, who was imprisoned and tortured by the Romanian authorities for a total of 14 years, inspired the founding of Release in 1968.

Richard Wurmbrand died in February 2001, but his vision and passion to serve persecuted Christians around the world continues in the ministry of Release today.

For further information, please contact:

Release International
PO Box 54
ORPINGTON
Kent
BR5 4RT

Tel: 01689 823491 Email: info@releaseinternational.org

or visit our website: www.releaseinternational.org

Daring Devotion

Paperback Edition 2017

Published by Release International

ISBN 978-0-9559693-2-4

COMMENDATIONS

I would highly recommend this book to anyone who is seeking to get closer to God.

One of the chapters focuses on forgiveness. This is an area I have really struggled with for nearly a year, after a major and very hurtful argument and fallout with my younger sister. We lost contact and it was eating me up not knowing how to deal with the situation. After reading the very emotive story in *Daring Devotion*, God very clearly spoke to me, telling me to end the uncomfortable silence. After I plucked up the courage to phone her in Australia we were able to put our differences aside and move on. This once again reminded me of God's amazing love for us and how things will happen at the time God decides.

M.G, Surrey

****

I enjoyed doing *Daring Devotion* because of the thematic approach, the inclusion of an individual's testimony and how each writer drew inspiration or insight from meeting that person.

There was enough in each chapter to spend more than one quiet time on the theme, or the personal reflection section.

I find visual content really helpful and illuminating for meditation and reflection so I liked the two visual aids - the Rembrandt *Prodigal* and the Korean artist's painting - very much...

Annie, Surrey

****

I found it very moving and deeply humbling to read of the circumstances of our Christian brothers and sisters in countries where presecution is rife. There are some remarkable accounts of grace, forgiveness and persistence all of which is very challenging for us in the West to know how to respond.

Derek, Kent

****

What a journey! So humbling, yet so inspiring.

Mike, Kent

****

Thank you for asking me to read *Daring Devotion*. I found it both moving and challenging.

John, Kent

****

DEDICATION

To Release International's faithful supporters who through their prayers and generosity have given hope and strength, and a voice, to persecuted Christians around the world since 1968.

CONTENTS

Message from Release International's Chief Executive

Thank you for buying this devotional. The funds raised from its sale will go towards helping persecuted Christians but it was not produced to make money. Its aim is to help you, a Christian in the 'free' world, to understand some of the lessons being learnt by believers around the world who are undergoing persecution. If we're honest we only know what we truly believe when our life is on the line. What does overcoming really look like, not as a concept but in practice? What does hope truly mean when your whole Christian life is spent behind bars? How do you cope with rejection when your close family try to kill you because you've chosen to follow Christ? These, and other subjects including faith, faithfulness and endurance, are all covered in this book. These topics are covered by many other publications, of course, and in more detail, but they are rarely approached from the point of view of Christians suffering persecution. I may know what faithfulness is in the light but do I know what it is in the dark, when my enemies surround me and my life's on the line? That's why we've called it *Daring Devotion* and my hope is that, from these devotions, you will be encouraged to use your freedom to become more of a daring disciple where you live and work, to the glory of God.

Each chapter has been written by someone connected to Release, either a staff member, volunteer or friend of our ministry. So, there is no single voice talking to you... except, we hope, the voice of God.

May God minister to you as you commit to *Daring Devotion*.

Paul Robinson

How to use *Daring Devotion*

If you are using this book for personal devotion, first, choose a quiet, comfortable space where you won't be interrupted. Then STOP! God says '*Be still* (stop) *and know that I am God*' (Psalm 46:10). Give yourself a few minutes to be quiet before God and recognise his presence and sovereignty in your life before you start each chapter. Then ask him to speak to you and minister to you as you read and respond. We recommend that you don't try to complete more than one session at a time so you can allow what God says to you to have the greatest impact. You might even want to repeat a chapter. Please take time to enjoy the creative input and the response and action sections. They are all part of gaining a fuller understanding.

Daring Devotion can also be used as a small group study guide. In fact its in-depth focus on themes rather than on providing daily inspiration makes it ideal for discussion.

If this book has helped you, then pass it on to someone else.

We'd love to receive your feedback too, so please email us at: info@releaseinternational.org

INTRODUCTION

We hear many stories every day: on the news, on social media, in the cinema. Some are true, others false, while some are designed to entertain and others to shock. What you will find included on the next pages, however, is more than just a collection of stories.

They are testimonies of persecuted Christians around the world. A testimony can be defined as 'evidence or proof of something' and they are indeed proof of something, the life to come that as Christians we long for.

What you are holding in your hands is a book bursting at the seams with hope. It contains proof of God's love, of how he relates to those who believe in him in every moment. It contains evidence of how he blesses the persecuted, people who stay faithful to him in the face of the gravest danger.

Compiling these testimonies was a learning process for me. I thought I knew what persecution looked like and how it might feel for those experiencing it, but then reading about what it can really mean to trust God with everything you have and are changed my ideas. So where I expected to feel sadness or fear, I felt encouragement and hope. Through the accounts of such brave people I have dared to hope more, to love more, to trust God more. I hope that as you read the testimonies and then reflect on and respond to what you've read, you will too.

Lisa-Marie Pusch
January 2017

Chapter 1
Forgiveness - Kenya

Creative input

'The Return of the Prodigal Son' by Rembrandt, c. 1669.

This is one of Rembrandt's last works. By painting a scene from Jesus' parable, the artist depicts a moment of repentance and forgiveness. Spend a few moments contemplating this painting of father and son, along with these words from Luke 15: 20 - 23.

'So he got up and went to his father. But while he was still a long way off, his father saw him and was filled with compassion for him; he ran to his son, threw his arms around him and kissed him. The son said to him, "Father, I have sinned against heaven and against you. I am no longer worthy to be called your son." But

the father said to his servants, "Quick! Bring the best robe and put it on him. Put a ring on his finger and sandals on his feet. Bring the fattened calf and kill it. Let's have a feast and celebrate. For this son of mine was dead and is alive again; he was lost and is found."
So they began to celebrate.'

Testimony

'I really forgive them from my heart because they are just human beings. I always pray that the living God will change their hearts and they will become born again and serve Him.' I mulled over these challenging words as I prepared to meet the woman who had spoken them to my colleague on an earlier visit to Kenya.

Kenyan Christian Sarah Ambetsa was widowed on March 23, 2014, when her church in Likoni (near Mombasa) was attacked by Islamist terrorists. Her husband, Philip, the assistant pastor, was murdered along with five other members of the congregation. Many others were injured, including Sarah.

It was 15 months later when I met Sarah in her small but robust house in a Kenyan slum which she shares with her two boys (Professor, who is six, and Jesse aged two) and other relatives. As the young children stared inquisitively at the strange visitor to their home, Sarah told me how life is a struggle. Apart from her ever-present grief, Sarah faces the difficulties of settling into a new city and providing for the needs of her family without her husband. She hopes to set up a small business selling second-hand clothes with a financial gift from supporters of Release International.

She was thankful that they have joined a good church nearby where the people are welcoming. Her oldest son is attending school and seems to enjoy it, although he still gets upset, understandably, if his mother ever has to visit Mombasa. The boys are quiet, only making a noise when they laugh at my pitiful attempts to count in Swahili.

Sarah was encouraged by the fact that her story had touched many of our supporters in the UK and Ireland. She was moved by the greetings cards they had written expressing their compassion and prayers for her. I told her that many people had remarked how her response to the attack revealed a deep faith and trust in God.

It was the same thing that struck me when I met Sarah, how she continues to acknowledge God's provision in all things. 'It is very hard sometimes but you have to just keep trusting in God,' she says. 'Everything is in his hands.' Sarah sees herself in terms of her relationship with God and not her circumstances. It would be very easy to be full of self-pity or to question God's care but she exuded a remarkable sense of calm and acceptance. I'm reminded of Sarah's reaction when she discovered that her husband had died. 'At that moment, I just told God, "He is yours and your name will be glorified." And I knew the living God would stand by me.' Whatever happens in her future, God is still sovereign; he is still her heavenly Father.

There was no anger or bitterness or sense of wanting revenge on those who committed the horrific act. She no doubt mourns the loss of her beloved husband and misses him greatly, but will not allow this to dictate how she thinks about her persecutors. We prayed together for her family's future, that God would continue to be at work in her life and support her as she raises her boys alone. Then we prayed for those who had attacked the church – not only that they would come to know Jesus as Lord and Saviour but that they would be blessed. These are requests that only God can make into our heart's desire for those who have harmed us.

Biblical reflection

When we hear stories like Sarah's, our natural response is

one of compassion and admiration, probably followed by the question, 'Would I be so willing to forgive if the same thing happened to me?' One of the ways our persecuted family challenge us is in showing genuine forgiveness to those who have harmed them.

What is genuine forgiveness?

We struggle with the concept of forgiveness as it can look as if we are dismissing the gravity of the offence or that we are implying that what happened was acceptable or that the wrong didn't matter. Yet, genuine forgiveness acknowledges the seriousness of the offence but chooses not to hold it against the perpetrator. It is admitting that it is not our place to judge and that we need to hand the judgment over to God.

Furthermore, it involves extending mercy to those who don't deserve it – to those who hate us and want to harm us. It is meeting their hatred with an attitude that refuses to seek retaliation but instead seeks their good. It is an attitude that reflects something of God's heart.

What God's forgiveness of us reveals about Him

God's forgiveness is not cheap. We are reminded in Romans 5:10 that it was while we were his enemies that Christ died for us to reconcile us to God. God did not wait for us to come to him or for us to ask to be forgiven before he acted for our good. It was while we were still set against him, living in rebellion, that he sent Jesus to pay the price for our sin, so that our relationship with him could be restored. God's forgiveness shows both the gravity of our sin and the extravagance of his love and grace.

What forgiving others reveals about us

Arguably the best-known verse about forgiveness in the Bible is found in the Lord's Prayer: '*and forgive us our sins, as we have forgiven those who sin against us.'* (Matthew 6:12 NLT). Forgiveness is an integral part of the prayer that Jesus taught us. Forgiveness should be central to our lives – both asking God for it and offering it to those who have wronged us.

Showing genuine and deep forgiveness is one of the distinguishing marks of a Christian. When we freely forgive others and hold no ill will towards them, we imitate Christ. The more we remember and experience God's overwhelming forgiveness, the more we will be willing to forgive others. This leads to radically distinctive behaviour where we not only forgive 'our enemies' but actively seek and pray for their good.

We know it's the right thing to do and we expect others to forgive us but it can be so hard to do when we have been personally affected. The world will tell us that we would be crazy to forgive those who have committed great wrongs against us – particularly wrongs of the magnitude that the extremists inflicted on Sarah. The world expects (if not encourages) us to nurse our hatred and seek our revenge on those who have wronged us. However, this is not an option for the Christian. Jesus warns us about refusing to forgive others, in the verses that come after the Lord's Prayer:

> *'For if you forgive other people when they sin against you,*
> *your heavenly Father will also forgive you.*
> *But if you do not forgive others their sins,*
> *your Father will not forgive your sins.'* (Matthew 6:14-15)

Our forgiveness from God is only because of Jesus' death and resurrection. Our forgiveness of others in no way contributes to our salvation but, if we are unwilling to forgive others, we have not understood the central message of the gospel. When we remember our total depravity and how undeserved God's mercy to us is, it should motivate us to have compassion and mercy towards others, whatever they have done and however hard it may be.

Speaking to Sarah about her experience and witnessing her attitude towards those who murdered her husband was extremely challenging. It reminded me that forgiveness is not just a sentimental or theological idea to which we should glibly adhere: instead, it's a fundamental part of our faith and a reality with which we often have to grapple. No doubt Sarah has to rely on God daily for the strength and grace to continue forgiving those whose actions have had very painful consequences for her. Yet, Sarah's continued willingness to show mercy is not because she is some kind of 'super Christian' who lives by unrealistic standards. Rather it is because she is motivated by the amazing forgiveness that every ordinary believer experiences from God.

Most of us will not have been called to show the extent of the forgiveness that Sarah has shown. But we will have all been hurt by someone's actions or words in the past and we all know the feelings of bitterness, anger and betrayal that can follow. It is a challenge for us to examine our own hearts to see if there is anyone or any situation where we are not truly deciding to forgive. If we find that we are holding on to bitterness and showing an unwillingness to forgive, we would do well to meditate on the wonder of God's incredible mercy towards us. When we remember the enormity of our sin against God and what it cost for us to be reconciled to him, it should put our grievances into perspective and encourage us to seek God's help to forgive others.

Response and action

You have just read Sarah's story and her thoughts and feelings about her enemies. Have you ever struggled with forgiveness? Whether you've already forgiven many enemies or never encountered animosity, write your own letter of forgiveness. It can be addressed to a real person or a fictitious one, or even be the words you would use if you were in Sarah's shoes. You do not need to send the letter; it is about trying to find the words to express forgiveness and to look for ways in which you can use them in everyday life.

If you want to encourage Sarah while she tries to support her family and remain forgiving, you can send her a card to let her know you are praying for her. To learn more about how this works, take a look at Release's 'Reach Out!' brochure which you can find on our website, www.releaseinternational.org

In a moment of quiet, reflect on this incredible truth from Psalm 86:5:

'You, Lord, are forgiving and good,
abounding in love to all who call to you.'

Chapter 2
Humility – Central Asia

Creative input

True humility is not an abject, grovelling, self-despising spirit; it is but a right estimate of ourselves as God sees us.
Tyron Edwards, 19th century teacher

'*God says when you are humble, you are free from pride and arrogance. You know that in your flesh you are inadequate, yet you also know who you are in Christ.*'
Doug Britton, author, 2014

Reflect on these quotes for a moment. Do they help define or explain humility for you or help you think of it in a different way? Who might you describe as humble? Why is that so? What do you learn from them and how they live that out?

Testimony

'*Humility is the fear of the Lord; its wages are riches and honour and life.*' (Proverbs 22:4)

It was the last visit of the day. We were emotionally exhausted. But, as we approached this house over the little foot-bridge in the dark of night, with only a small torch to guide us, I had no idea of the impact that meeting this family would have on my walk with God. We were invited to sit at the low table, spread with an array of traditional food. Our hosts, Constantin (not his real name) and his wife, know the cost of following Jesus

Christ. They had been born into a devout Muslim family but, after hearing the gospel of Jesus Christ, they decided to follow him. To leave Islam and to follow Christ in Central Asia can mean being ostracised by the entire family.

Persecution did come, initially from their Muslim family: Constantin's mother, believing that they had brought shame on their family, decided to shame her son and daughter-in-law by throwing herself into the river. Thankfully, her attempt to drown herself failed as a local fisherman spotted her and pulled her out. She then gathered the village leaders together and demanded that her son and his wife attend this meeting. The whole village was against them. Constantin's wife was terrified so he went on his own to face the mob. He knew God was with him as, miraculously, one man stood up to defend him. He asked Constantin's mother why she was against her hard-working, respectable son. She was so offended by this that she moved to another village.

Constantin and his family were persecuted by others in the village. Nobody spoke to them; the bus driver stopped picking the children up for school. The children were beaten several times at school so had to stop going. For a whole year, Constantin's wife cried and cried – the persecution and isolation were taking their toll. Each morning she would cry and each morning Constantin would say, 'Here is the word of God, read it and stand on its promises.' When his nephew died, they went to the funeral but at the graveside people threw stones at them. Their relatives wouldn't speak to them as they believed the nephew had died because Constantin and his wife had turned their back on Islam.

For five years, they faced persecution, but day by day their faith in God grew. They continued to trust God; they remained faithful to his word. They showed grace, love and humility. Eventually, their family members began, one by one, to show respect. Several relatives chose to follow Christ, including Constantin's mother. They still have difficulties but in their own words, 'We see God's glory. We were left with nothing and now God has blessed us so much. We have prosperity and respect, yes, respect even from the Government and police.' God has given them back the material things which they had lost as a result of following him – and they use them for his glory by opening up their home to feed the homeless. They provide the finance for much of the church's outreach into the Muslim community.

What a blessing to meet this family. I felt I was witnessing a story of God's power and presence equal to the stories in the book of Acts. I was humbled by their faith. I was so moved that, instead of offering to pray for them, I asked them to pray for us, for the church in the 'free' West, where secularism and materialism often dilute our faith in God.

Biblical reflection

'All of you, clothe yourselves with humility toward one another, because, "God opposes the proud but shows favour to the humble." Humble yourselves, therefore, under God's mighty hand, that he may lift you up in due time. Cast all your anxiety on him because he cares for you.' (1 Peter 5:5-7)

In Constantin and his family, I had met believers who lived out these verses. The truth of God's word was evident in their attitude to their persecutors. They saw their story as evidence of God working out his promise. They had cast all their anxiety on him and he had cared for them. Their humility was evident as they told their story.

We saw them as giants of faith; they saw themselves as servants of God trying to imitate Christ's humility.

'If you have any encouragement from being united with Christ, if any comfort from his love, if any fellowship with the Spirit, if any tenderness and compassion, then make my joy complete by being like-minded, having the same love, being one in spirit and purpose. Do nothing out of selfish ambition or vain conceit, but in humility consider others better than yourselves. Each of you should look not only to your own interests, but also to the interests of others. Your attitude should be the same as that of Christ Jesus: Who, being in very nature God, did not consider equality with God something to be grasped, but made himself nothing, taking the very nature of a servant, being made in human likeness. And being found in appearance as a man, he humbled himself and became obedient to death – even death on a cross!' (Philippians 2:1-8)

Jesus humbled himself when he came as a baby, as the Son of God, to a lowly birth in a dirty stable. He humbled himself when he, in total obedience to his father, died on the cross. We are to imitate Christ. Our attitude should be that of Christ. We are to obey and to trust our God, knowing encouragement from our walk with him and showing his love to others. This is so different to what the world expects of us. For example, we may feel we need to promote ourselves, to walk over anyone who gets in the way of us getting to where we want to go or where we think we deserve to be. But, if we are humble we put God first and trust him to guide us and equip us and to encourage others as we serve him.

A humble person is not a 'doormat', not someone that allows others to walk all over them. A humble person is someone who has confidence in God and in what God can and will do through them.

'Therefore, as God's chosen people, holy and dearly loved, clothe yourselves with compassion, kindness, humility, gentleness and patience.' (Colossians 3:12)

Both 1 Peter and Colossians tell us to 'clothe ourselves'. We are to wear humility, putting it on daily and appropriately. As clothes are necessary for our physical body so humility is necessary for our spiritual body. Like our clothes, it should be evident to others.

In our humility, we acknowledge God as the source of all that is good in life. A humble person will give God the glory. In hard times, in difficult circumstances, in our humility we know that God will not let us down. We see that in Constantin's faith-based humility. But humility is also seen when life is good, through our thankfulness. We are to be thankful in all circumstances, knowing that God is working out his purposes. Romans 8:28 tells us: '*And we know that in all things God works for the good of those who love him, who have been called according to his purpose.*'

As well as giving continual thanks to God in all circumstances, humility appreciates people. We are to tell people that we appreciate their help and encouragement. We are not to take others for granted. The world tells us we deserve to be treated well, but a humble person expresses their gratitude to God and to those who God has blessed them with, to their family and friends. We are to show thankfulness and express thankfulness to those around us. Paul in 1 Thessalonians 5:16-18 says, '*Rejoice always, pray continually, give thanks in all circumstances; for this is God's will for you in Christ Jesus.*'

Response and action

Constantin shared that, at times, the decision to follow Christ meant he lost everything, including the ability to provide for his family. It is only a very humble man who accepts that and looks to God for his provision.

You can pray for Christians such as Constantin and the

others featured in this book but you can also help them practically. Supporters of Release have held events such as curry evenings for their church home groups during which they've shown DVDs about persecuted Christians to encourage prayer and to raise awareness and even financial support for projects. One particular Release event for women is the Esther Experience, an evening of pampering your friends while at the same time telling others about persecuted Christian women. You could, for example, open your house for friends to share some simple beauty treatments as they discuss the story of Esther from the Old Testament in a relaxed, friendly environment. If you feel it's appropriate you may wish to charge a small entry fee or ask for a donation towards work helping Christians like those mentioned in this book.

We'd love to hear how you get on so please feel free to email us with a short report and any photos of your event to info@releaseinternational.org

To see a list of DVDs that you can use at an event visit our website at www.releaseinternational.org

Chapter 3
Redemption - Pakistan

Creative input

The only interest I gained in classical music was when I sang in the school choir. I'll never forget the buzz as a 12-year-old singing in an ancient church, rehearsing with other schools a piece from Handel's Messiah called 'I know that my Redeemer liveth'. It gave me goose bumps as my young, inexperienced, wobbly notes contributed to a crescendo of sound that sounded surprisingly beautiful!

'I know that my Redeemer liveth
And that He shall stand at the latter day upon the earth.
And tho' worms destroy this body
Yet in my flesh shall I see God.
I know that my Redeemer liveth:
For now is Christ risen from the dead,
the first fruits of them that sleep.'

I did not understand the sentiments of those words from the book of Job at the time. Understanding only came four years later when, as a new believer, I sang 'There is a Redeemer', by Melody and Keith Green.

'There is a redeemer,
Jesus, God's own Son,
Precious Lamb of God,
Messiah,
Holy One.'

Redeemer? By the time I sang these words, Keith Green and two of his children had been killed in a plane crash. However, Melody was still singing this song and sharing that message, even while living with pain and loss. Jesus the Redeemer had not only saved her but even redeemed some of her own tragic story. Melody continues in ministry and worship to this day, leading and inspiring others through their own tragedies.

Testimony

I met Noreen in a dusty yard in Pakistan. I had been showered with welcoming rose petals as I entered the sewing centre – the traditional celebration given to visitors. After the welcome dance, with more honour bestowed on me in the form of garlands of sweet scented flowers, I was introduced to Noreen, a woman whose life and light seemed to have left her eyes and her whole being. There was I, a focus of celebration, and she a woman in deep pain and anguish. Quickly I removed the garlands, held her hand gently and listened to the translation.

Two weeks ago, she and her husband had been at work. They had left their two children at home as they did not have relatives nearby to take care of them. The eight-year-old daughter looked after her younger brother aged five. They lived as Christians in a village alongside Muslim neighbours. Noreen's husband had recently sold a buffalo and had left the cash hidden in the house ready to buy what they needed. Their Muslim neighbour, a taxi driver, had broken into the house to try to steal the money. He seemed not to expect the children to be there and they caught him in the act. To cover up his crime, he strangled them both with a cord, wrapped them in the seat cover of his taxi and dumped their bodies in a ditch outside the village.

On her return from work, Noreen searched for her children with growing desperation. Eventually, someone found the bodies. The seat cover they were wrapped in was recognised as being from the neighbour's taxi and used as evidence against him. He was arrested and taken to the police station.

What justice is there for a Christian family against a Muslim man with contacts and influence? The suspect was released after two days. And he simply moved back next-door to Noreen. Did they have the resources to appeal or build a case? No. Did they have the confidence to speak out for themselves? No. They even turned down the offer of a safe house, such was their sense of powerlessness and grief.

I just held Noreen's hand and prayed and said that I would be committed to sharing her story so others might pray as well.

Biblical reflection

Noreen and her husband must have felt as though they had lost everything, just as Job had lost everything: his status, wealth, family, well-being and even the understanding and empathy of his so called 'comforters'. Yet he wrote this:

'I know that my Redeemer lives,
and that in the end he will stand on the earth.
And after my skin has been destroyed,
yet in my flesh I will see God.' (Job 19:25-26)

Read Job 19.

Look for the way verse 25 leaps out amid the torment, the abandonment and the heart-breaking cries of a man completely misunderstood by those close to him. Job: blameless, upright, a man who feared God and yet was tormented now by evil. But verse 25 is a 'brilliant flash of faith', as one commentator writes. Job uses the word 'redeemer' with purpose. Translated to Hebrew, it is *goel*, which stands for one who defends another person unjustly accused of wrong. A 'redeemer' would stand alongside someone suffering through no fault of their own. For example, if someone had lost land or money through a relative dying, a redeemer was able to give them the chance of a new beginning. A 'redeemer' was seen as an advocate, someone with the power to 'buy you back'. Job declared that he knew **the** Redeemer and that he was living and active!

To know his God with such confidence amid an outpouring and experience of pain is an incredible witness in a man who had dedicated his life to knowing God. Think what had contributed towards such knowledge of God. Study, dedication and sacrifice, as well as living a full and successful life until it was taken from him (see Job 1). It was this foundation that had brought him to this moment and the realisation that his God is living and active, even amid his own suffering and pain.

As an Old Testament figure, Job did not know Jesus. If you have turned your life to Christ, you do know him and are now able to see the full magnitude of Job's words. C. H. Spurgeon wrote:

'Remember, too, that it was always considered to be the duty of the goel, not merely to redeem by price, but where that failed, to redeem by power... There are two redemptions, – redemption by price and redemption by power, and both of these Christ hath wrought for us; – by price, by his sacrifice upon the cross of Calvary; and by power, by his Divine Spirit coming into our heart, and renewing our soul.'

Response and action

Ask yourself:

- What foundation of faith do I have that I can build upon when suffering and pain come?
- What have I done or said to God and to others when I struggle and endure? Does it reflect Job and his witness to me?

- How well do I *know* God?
- What am I doing to build knowledge, wisdom and faith?

An update on Noreen's story...

I met Noreen again, 15 months later. She grinned at me through a sea of faces and I recognised her immediately. In her arms, I saw a sleeping baby. Without anything being said it was apparent that God had stepped in. He had not replaced the children she had lost, but he had blessed her with a new son.

God had acted in power and compassion as the Redeemer. Noreen explained to me over lunch that she had cried out for justice for her children to God. She felt she could do nothing herself – but that her Father God could. Then in a dream God spoke to her very clearly. She saw him bringing a cradle filled with a baby to bless her and he said to her three times, 'I will be judge, I will be judge, I will be judge.' When she woke, she shared the dream with her husband and since then, though desperately poor and still living in a hostile place, they have lived in that promise. Even though justice might not be theirs on earth, he will bring justice. For Jesus the Redeemer, the Advocate, the Defender, *the Goal* is living and alive in them and for them. He will judge the living and the dead as he redeems the whole earth.

For we know that our Redeemer lives!

Listen to one of the following songs (all can be found on YouTube):

- Keith Green: *'There is a Redeemer'*
- Handel: *'I know that my Redeemer liveth'*
- Big Daddy Weave: *'Redeemed'*

Reflect on the power of redemption in your life through

Jesus, your Redeemer.

Listen to the song again.

Ask what God would want you to do on behalf of Noreen and others like her. How will you now pray for her and our persecuted family? How will their testimony shape your faith?

Write your response on the cradle below.

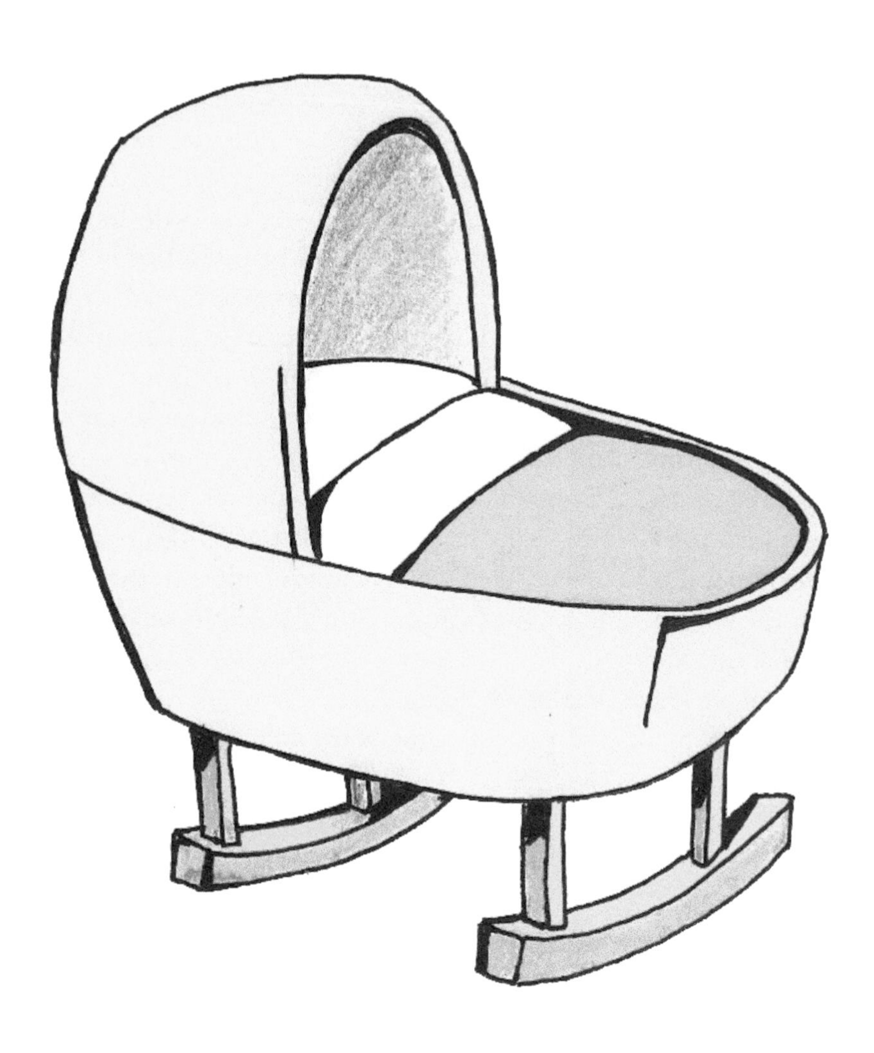

Chapter 4
Faithfulness – Iran

Creative input

Look at these backpacks; spend a few minutes considering what thoughts and words come to mind as you look at them before reading any further.

Travelling? Burdens? Holidays? Suicide bombers? Adventures? Picnics? Some of these perhaps and many others too I expect, but probably not the word 'faithfulness'. Why then do these backpacks remind me of faithfulness?

Testimony

It's because the backpacks I'm thinking of belonged to two Iranian Christians, Maryam Rostampour (pictured left overleaf) and Marziyeh Amirizadeh (right).

Their faces are instantly recognisable to many, for these young women were imprisoned in Iran's notorious Evin prison in 2009 for sharing their faith in Christ. These two women have paid a high price for their faithfulness to God and yet they testify to God's unfailing faithfulness to them. Part of their testimony is also about the faithfulness of Christian brothers and sisters around the world who campaigned for their release.

Two years ago, I had the privilege of meeting Maryam and Marziyeh during their visit to the UK. During a meeting in a committee room at Portcullis House in Parliament, the women shared about the circumstances that had led to their arrest, their imprisonment and their subsequent release.

Maryam and Marziyeh met when they were studying theology in Turkey, having previously converted from Islam, and they formed a strong friendship. When they returned to Iran after their studies, they felt inspired by God to share their passion for Jesus and for their country by distributing New Testaments throughout Tehran. They knew the dangers this posed and they heard rumours that the authorities were worried about a large organisation distributing Christian literature. But Maryam and Marziyeh knew it was not a large organisation: in their own words, it was just two girls with two backpacks!

That phrase, 'just two girls with two backpacks', has stayed with me. The girls believed that they had been inspired by God to distribute New Testaments throughout the city and they were obedient to his call to do so, demonstrating their trust and faith in him, knowing that their actions could have serious consequences for them, their families and friends. They didn't need expensive equipment and training; they needed to be faithful with the gifts they had: their belief in Jesus Christ as their Saviour and their desire to see others come to know him, along with a stack of New Testaments and two backpacks.

Recently, I've been studying the life of Jesus' disciple Peter, an ordinary Galilean fisherman, as rough and ready as they come. But Jesus took him as he was; he used Peter's skills in fishing and taught him to become a fisher of men. When he sent out Peter and the other 11 disciples, he sent them out two by two in his authority, with little equipment and just a few instructions (Luke 9:1-6). But Matthew's account of this event also includes a warning for the disciples, that they were to be on their guard against men who would hand them over to the ruling authorities and that they would be arrested. But Jesus also promised that the Spirit would give them the words to say (Matthew 10:17-20). The disciples were obedient to Jesus' command and they went out to preach the gospel and heal the sick. Before long, they had attracted the attention of the ruling authority in the region, Herod the tetrarch. The disciples do not appear to have been arrested on that occasion, for when they returned to Jesus they were eager to tell him all that they had done, but they must have been aware that it had been a strong possibility (Luke 9:7-9).

Maryam and Marziyeh are as different from Peter as it is possible to be! They are beautiful, well-educated women, with warm and engaging personalities. Just as God used the rough and ready fisherman Peter and the other disciples, so too he used these women and their abilities and gifts; he sent them out 'two by two' with their backpacks. Maybe they even felt like two of the 12 being sent out, with Jesus' words of warning ringing in their ears! As they went, they knew God's protection and guidance on them each day as they trekked the streets, distributing Bibles and taking every God-given opportunity to evangelise during three years which they describe as 'exhausting and exhilarating'. They were being faithful to God and obedient to his command to them, just as the disciples were. Despite this, in March 2009, they too attracted the attention of the ruling authorities and what was perhaps inevitable happened: the women were arrested.

Had God abandoned them, despite their faithfulness to him?

At first glance, it may seem so, but Maryam and Marziyeh would say otherwise. They realised that, for the couple of months before their arrest, they had not been able to evangelise, for reasons they couldn't explain; neither had they been able to distribute a single New Testament. They hadn't realised that the police were watching them and, if they had met with people as usual during those two months of being observed, many more people would have been arrested: this was God's faithfulness at work. They had been imprisoned, but many others had been protected.

Surely though, in prison, they could no longer be faithful in obedience to God? The story I heard the women share in fluent English in a British parliamentary office proved otherwise. The women may no longer have had the opportunity to take the gospel out and to distribute it literally from their backpacks but now, in prison, they had a captive audience. They had prayed for years for opportunities to share their faith and now their prison became their church. Here, the women had the freedom to talk to their fellow prisoners about why they were there and they praised God for giving them such an opportunity! In their cold, dark and terrifying 'church', as they faced the mental torture of expecting to be executed, they saw many people come to Christ; even some of the guards asked them to pray for them. Being imprisoned changed Maryam and Marziyeh's view; they understood then that everywhere can be a church, even a dark and brutal place such as Evin prison. God hadn't abandoned them – he had answered their prayers in the most amazing way. Their circumstances may have changed, but God's faithfulness to them had not. Throughout their time in prison, Maryam and Marziyeh refused to give up their belief or to recant their faith and during their 259 days of detention, God demonstrated his faithfulness to them over and over again.

The women knew God's faithfulness but they felt, as they faced the terrors of prison life, that they had been forgotten – not by God, but by the outside world. Forgotten, that is, until they heard that many Christians had sent them letters and cards, as well as writing to the authorities on their behalf. Maryam and Marziyeh firmly believe that the letters made a difference; they made the authorities change their behaviour towards them and ultimately they contributed to their release. If we have ever wondered if the letters and cards we write to our persecuted brothers and sisters make a difference, especially those in prison, or if the letters of advocacy we write to the authorities on behalf of others have an impact, here is our answer. The faithfulness of other believers, obedient to God's command in Hebrews 13:3 to 'remember those in prison', had a significant impact on their situation, leading eventually to their release.

Maryam and Marziyeh are now living in America and are

studying international law so that they can advocate for their brothers and sisters in Iran who still suffer. They continue to be faithful servants of the Lord and they are fulfilling the promise that they made to their fellow prisoners, that they would be a voice for them.

Maryam and Marziyeh's full story can be read in *Captive in Iran*, published by Tynedale Momentum.

Biblical reflection

The Bible is full of stories of God's faithfulness; think of Moses or Joseph, of Elizabeth or Mary. The Psalms particularly resonate with words proclaiming the faithfulness of the Lord. Songs fill our churches on Sunday mornings that echo similar words and sentiments. All this is good and Maryam and Marziyeh have personal testimony of God's faithfulness, but what's the reality of God's faithfulness to each of us in our own lives? Let's return to Peter and consider how God's faithfulness was evident in his life and reflect on how it is evident in our own.

God demonstrated his faithfulness to Peter right from the moment of his calling. Having fished all night, Peter, the experienced fisherman, had returned with his crew empty-handed. But he placed his trust in Jesus from the outset and let down his nets again, only to have them overwhelmed with so many fish that the boats began to sink (Luke 5:1-11). What an assurance to Peter that God would be faithful in his material provision for him, enabling Peter to leave everything and follow him. We're not all called to 'leave everything' but we can trust in God that he will provide for us as we seek to follow his will in our daily lives. Many of us are understandably anxious about earning a decent living or making ends meet. God knows this, just as he knew Peter's concerns. Maryam and Marziyeh had to be entirely dependent on God during their imprisonment and to trust in his faithfulness to them. We too need to continue to trust in God's faithfulness to us in all things, and especially as *Jehovah Jireh*, our provider.

To me, one of the most memorable accounts from Peter's life is when he walked on water. Out on a boat on the Sea of Galilee in familiar surroundings late at night, the disciples saw the far from familiar sight of a figure walking on the water towards them. Fearing it was a ghost, they cried out and Jesus' reassuring voice bounced back to them, exhorting them to take courage. Peter, true to his impetuous character, immediately wanted to walk out to meet Jesus and he responded to Jesus' command, 'Come', by stepping out of the boat onto the water. Only when he took his eyes off Jesus and noticed the wind did he begin to sink. In his desperation, he called out to Jesus to save him and Jesus reached out his hand and caught him. Peter wavered momentarily in his faith as the reality of his situation hit him and he doubted (Matthew 14:22-33). How often has that happened to us? We step out to do something for God but then feel overwhelmed and defeated by the task in hand. What's our response? Do we plough on and try to overcome difficulties alone or do we cry out to Jesus as Peter did? Jesus is waiting to reach out to us; he understands our doubts. What was the outcome of this incident? It caused those in the boat to *worship* Jesus. I am sure there would have been times when Maryam and Marziyeh had momentary doubts, especially during their time in prison, just as we may do at times in our lives; our faithfulness may waver, but God's never will.

We may look at people such as Maryam and Marziyeh as spiritual heroes for enduring persecution for their faith; we may think of Peter as a spiritual giant. But Maryam and Marziyeh are ordinary young women, just as Peter was an ordinary man; we too are just ordinary people. I am sure that Maryam and Marziyeh would be the first to admit that there have been occasions in their lives when they have got things wrong. I know I have, and we know without doubt that Peter did, in spectacular fashion! Having had the remarkable insight into who Jesus was and confessing him as '*Christ, the son of the living God*' (Matthew 16:16 KJV); having spent three years with Jesus, learning and ministering alongside Him; having promised at the Last Supper that he would never disown Jesus but would die with him if necessary (Matthew 26:35), Peter should have understood all there was to know about faithfulness. Instead, in a moment of crisis, when his world was being torn apart, he denies even knowing Christ, three times. When the cock crows and the reality of what he has just done hits him, Peter, the hardy fisherman, breaks down and weeps bitterly (Matthew 26:75). He got it about as wrong as it is possible to do. When he needed God most, he rejected him. Have we done the same? When we are torn apart through crisis, family breakdown, illness, bereavement, redundancy?

Peter may have rejected Jesus and abandoned God, but God in his eternal faithfulness did not abandon him. Jesus took the very first opportunity after his resurrection to reveal his faithfulness to Peter again. First by providing another remarkable catch of fish - how that must have stirred a memory in Peter! And secondly, and much more personally, by giving Peter three opportunities to state how much he loved Jesus. Three denials wiped away by three declarations of love; a re-issued command to Peter to 'Follow me'. God's faithfulness prevailed and Peter went on to be key to spreading the gospel of Christ and to establishing the church.

God did not abandon Maryam and Marziyeh in prison; God did not abandon Peter despite his failings. God does not, and will not, abandon us - his faithfulness is not dependent on us, what we do, how good we are; it is part of his character. Paul teaches us in Romans 3:3 that people's lack of faith does not nullify God's faithfulness. Peter, like Maryam and Marziyeh, learnt what it meant to be persecuted for following Christ, as we read in Acts. We may never experience persecution like that, but we can learn to trust in him and his faithfulness to us and to grow in our faith and faithfulness to him in every aspect of our lives.

Response and action

Spend a few minutes reflecting on these two verses of scripture which speak of God's faithfulness.

> *'Know therefore that the LORD your God is God: he is the faithful God, keeping his covenant of love to a thousand generations of those who love him and keep his commandments.'* (Deuteronomy 7:9)

> *'God is faithful, who has called you into fellowship with his Son, Jesus Christ our Lord.'* (1 Corinthians 1:9)

Now, consider again the backpacks at the beginning of this chapter, which I described as a symbol of faithfulness. In one of them, imagine that you are putting all the things that you have thought, said or done that showed your lack of faithfulness to God. Confess these things, repent of them and then 'give' the backpack to God to take it away forever.

In the other rucksack, 'place' all the ways that God has shown his faithfulness to you, all the things that he has done for you, all that he has taught you, revealed to you, the scriptures you know that demonstrate his faithfulness to you. 'Take' this rucksack with you to dip into on your journey with him, as an encouragement and a reminder, wherever your journey may take you and whatever you may encounter on the way; and echo the words of the Psalmist as you go:

'Whoever dwells in the shelter of the Most *High will rest in the shadow of the* Almighty. *I will say of the Lord,*
"He is my refuge and my fortress,
my God, *in whom I trust."*
Surely he will save you from the fowler's
snare and from the deadly pestilence.
He will cover you with his feathers,
and under his wings you will find refuge;
his ***faithfulness*** (my emphasis)
will be your shield and rampart.' (Psalm 91:1-4)

Chapter 5
Endurance – India

Creative input

As you read these two excerpts below, spend a few moments considering the contrast between the sentiments expressed. Which best reflects your viewpoint?

Out of the night that covers me,
Black as the pit from pole to pole,
I thank whatever gods may be
For my unconquerable soul.

In the fell clutch of circumstance
I have not winced nor cried aloud.
Under the bludgeonings of chance
My head is bloody, but unbowed.

Beyond this place of wrath and tears
Looms but the Horror of the shade,
And yet the menace of the years
Finds, and shall find me, unafraid.

It matters not how strait the gate,
How charged with punishments the scroll,

I am the master of my fate:
I am the captain of my soul.

'Invictus' by William Henley

Should nothing of our efforts stand
No legacy survive
Unless the Lord does raise the house
In vain the builders strive

To you who boast tomorrow's gain,
Tell me what is your life?
A mist that vanishes at dawn
All glory be to Christ.

All glory be to Christ, our King!
All glory be to Christ!
His rule and reign we'll ever sing,
All glory be to Christ!

First verses of 'All glory be to Christ' by Kings Kaleidoscope

Testimony

Pastor John Lazarus has seen God work in some amazing ways, in and through his life. He and his family have also endured great suffering for their Lord.

His story is yet another powerful testimony to the amazing grace of God – but also a distinct and profound challenge to us to consider what it means to *persevere* in the Christian life.

John comes from the southern part of India. Like most Indians, he is from a Hindu background. In recent years there have been many testimonies of Indians from the lower castes, and particularly from a 'Dalit' background, hearing the gospel and coming to a liberating discovery of their true value as sinners who have been redeemed in the Lord Jesus. John, however, comes from an upper-caste Hindu background. This means that socially and culturally he was in a position to enjoy the privileges of the Indian way of life.

John's story of coming to faith in Christ begins in the most unpromising of circumstances. It began when his wife developed an unhealthy interest in the occult – something John refers to pointedly as 'witchcraft'. Such things are not uncommon in India. Hinduism is, in many ways, a broad cultural religion that has a tendency to embrace and absorb all manner of 'spiritual practices'. The 'dark side' of such practices are often seen when people are confronted with the truth of the gospel and the reality of Jesus Christ.

God, however, was at work and he led John's wife out of her occult practices. John simply says: 'She was healed.' It was around this time that he himself came to a saving faith in the Lord Jesus Christ.

The Lord quickly led John into active Christian service, and he began a prayer meeting in his own home. Later he built a small, dedicated prayer room at his house.

It was at this point that John began to experience opposition from local Hindus, seemingly determined to put an end to his gospel ministry. Members of the Rashtriya Swayamsevak Sangh (RSS) organisation attacked and ransacked his home. The RSS (the name is usually translated as 'National Volunteer Organisation') is a leading Hindu nationalist movement in India, dedicated to promoting Hindu supremacy.

John continued to develop his gospel work. A couple of years later, his family was attacked and his 18-year-old son, Satyan, was stabbed to death. His daughter, Manohari, who was in her 20s at the time, was abducted. Despite a frantic search by John, his family and friends, his daughter was never found.

Release International's partner in India said the violent attack and abduction were a clear warning to John to stop his gospel work.

But he didn't. Instead, by the grace of God, he *persevered* in the work to which he felt the Lord had called him. Since the assault on his family, John has himself been attacked twice. When he started a new church, he was set upon and beaten up by a man who, like John, was an upper-caste Hindu. He told me he has forgiven that man. It was at this point that Release's partner began supporting and resourcing John's ministry.

Despite all the opposition John has faced, he continues his gospel work. Moreover, he has another son who has also become a Christian minister! His story is a remarkable testimony to Christian perseverance, by the grace of God.

When I met him, I could see in this man a resoluteness and an evident, deep-seated joy, fashioned by the trials and tribulations he has faced since coming to faith in Jesus Christ.

Despite what he has been through, I saw no trace either of self-pity or of malice towards those who have opposed him and have inflicted great suffering on him and his family. Instead, by the grace of God, I could see a wonderful determination to go on serving the Lord who had saved him.

After we had heard his story, and the sequence of trials and afflictions he and his family had faced over the years, we naturally wanted to pray for him – and we did so. But how humbling it was when we were told by our translator that *he wanted to pray for us*. And so he did. He knelt by the table in the room where we met and prayed for us and for the ministry of Release International to persecuted Christians.

Biblical reflection

At a pivotal moment in his letter to the Christians in Rome, Paul writes:

'Therefore, since we have been justified by faith, we have peace with God through our Lord Jesus Christ. Through him we have also obtained access by faith into this grace in which we stand, and we rejoice in hope of the glory of God. More than that, we rejoice in our sufferings, knowing that suffering produces endurance, and endurance produces character, and character produces hope, and hope does not put us to shame, because God's love has been poured into our hearts through the Holy Spirit who has been given to us.' (Romans 5:1-5 ESV).

The word 'Therefore' at the beginning of this paragraph naturally links what Paul is about to say with what has gone before: a conclusion is being drawn on the basis of what has already been said. We are driven back, then, to grasp the message of the previous section of the letter (Romans 3:21 - 4:25) in which Paul has comprehensively set out the gospel: the good news that God puts people right with himself ('justifies' them) through faith in the saving, sacrificial work of Jesus Christ on the cross.

The fruit of this gift of justification is 'peace with God'. The context makes clear that 'peace' here is not tranquillity - it is about *relationship with God*. Peace is not 'chilling on the patio on a sunny Sunday afternoon' (nice though that might be!) Peace is a status we enjoy permanently, of being reconciled to God when once we were his enemies (to use the language of Romans 5:10-

11). This status of being justified is abiding and immovable, and enables us to look forward with a certain hope to sharing in the eternal glory of God (Romans 5:2).

So far so good. But then Paul makes a remarkable statement: '*Not only that, but we rejoice in our sufferings...*' (Romans 5:3 ESV). Our attitude to present suffering is to be the same as our attitude to the future hope of glory! How can that be?

The sufferings that Paul has in mind here are almost certainly the sufferings that come our way in this life *because* we are Christians. This includes persecution (see Romans 8:17-18). Such sufferings provide occasions for the grace of God to be seen, and so for God to be glorified (e.g. 2 Corinthians12:9).

Here in Romans 5 the focus is on what we might describe as the 'character-building' aspect of suffering for Christ. Notice how the process brings us full circle: In Romans 5:2 we 'rejoice' in the hope we have of eternal glory (knowing we are justified before God); in verses 4 and 5 the perseverance and character that flow from the suffering we endure bring us back to this hope we have! This hope is grounded in the love God has shown us (in his Son); something that is sealed in us by the Holy Spirit.

We rejoice, then, in our suffering for Christ, says Paul, not because we are masochists, nor because we want to 'play the hero'. Rather, the perseverance that such suffering calls for fixes our spiritual eyes more clearly on our eternal hope (see 1 Peter 4:12-14, where Peter makes a similar point). This hope should shape every facet of the present life we live.

In the lives of people like Pastor John Lazarus, we see evidence of the reality of Paul's teaching.

Response and action

1. How can the testimonies of persecuted Christians today be an encouragement to us?

2. In the light of Romans 5:1-5, what would you say is the

most important thing to pray for when we pray for persecuted Christians today?

3. Read Romans 8:16-39. Paul says more about suffering for Christ in this next section of his letter. But what is the overarching point being made here? Use these verses to pray for your own perspective on life and for your persecuted brothers and sisters.

MY

Chapter 6
Faith – North Korea

Creative input

Please read Mrs Bae's story below a couple of times. Firstly, to understand the situation and the context and then secondly, putting yourself in the speaker's shoes. How does it feel? Imagine: what faith does it take to go on such a journey?

Mrs Bae from North Korea says:

'My name is Mrs Bae and I am not brave. But I believe in a God, Emmanuel: God with us. God will be our navigator, I told my daughter and my even younger son as we packed up our home in North Korea, for the very last time. He will be our Guide, little ones, I told them.

We would go to China to follow my husband, Mr Bae, who had already defected almost a year before us. We packed just a few possessions and some travel documents and away we went.

We walked all day, every day, sometimes through snowdrifts packed chest-high. I didn't know whether we would survive, my young pregnant daughter and my little boy. How would we make it? Who would we cry out to, with no husband by our side? But we did cry out; we cried out to God, who walked with us like the risen Jesus walked with the disciples on the road to Emmaus. Every day, we walked with him. Every day, a miracle of hospitality came from the North Korean people. We stick together, you see, we North Koreans, we always have and we always do. We stick together. Even when we are hungry, even when we are starving, we practise hospitality. It goes deep, deep within culture long ago.

I looked at the mountains, the North Korean mountains that stood almost as powerful a guard as the sentries in the North Korean police. Would we make it to China? We hid in trucks packed full of rice. We even treated the sick, my pregnant daughter and I. Many people we stayed with were so poorly that we treated them, in exchange for gifts and even money.

But one day I realised that that money would not be enough for any border-pass we might need. We would have to swim for our lives. Swim, with a pregnant daughter and a little son. Swim through icy water. Emmanuel, God with us.

My little son jumped first and then my daughter. Seven months pregnant, she jumped into the icy water. She cried out to me: 'Mama, God can be trusted!' as she jumped. And then I followed suit.

Behind us, a life in North Korea; an impenetrable darkness. But as we swam there were gunshots. Gunshots, hard on our heels. People shouting out: 'Catch them, Catch them!'

I prayed: 'Lord, will we survive this?' And then, as we swam, almost faint, we saw the Christmas lights twinkling in the bay of China. Christmas lights! Emmanuel, God with us.

We made it; my daughter, my grandchild not yet born, and my little boy. Three generations, safe to live for Jesus. Three generations that would tell a story of hope and of the dignity and goodness of our God; and of our nation, North Korea. The light shines in the darkness and the darkness will never overcome it!'

Passage written by Judy Moore, adapted from *These are the Generations* by Mr and Mrs Bae, as told to Rev Eric Foley.

Testimony

On a trip to South Korea, I had the privilege of meeting North Korean defectors and hearing their stories. As I learnt about the awful conditions they'd left behind, the perilous 3,000-mile journey to safety and the not-so-easy life they now lead in South Korea, I marvelled at their faith.

The North Koreans had not left their country lightly: people only leave when they are desperate, their lives in danger. This may be through starvation or because their faith has been discovered. We met the son of a North Korean evangelist. His mother had told him to flee when she heard that the security forces were coming for them, but she herself was captured and shot by firing squad for refusing to stop sharing her faith. It was so important to her that she felt it worth dying for. This made me wonder: how much are we prepared to risk to share our faith? Who could we reach out to who needs to hear the gospel of good news?

Many of the North Koreans we met had found Jesus on their journey. They had been taught to have faith in the 'system' and their Great Leader back in North Korea, but soon realised that what they had been taught was not true. Those who sheltered the North Koreans in China showed them the love of Christ and shared their faith with them. Yet again, this means risking life, as the Chinese Government has an agreement with North Korea to send back any defectors who are discovered in China. It is labour camps and death for any escapees brought to the attention of the Chinese authorities. The North Korean policy is to punish to the third generation if one person shames the nation by defecting.

One lady led four hundred people to Christ while she was being held as a North Korean Defector in prison in Thailand, waiting to be allowed to go on to South Korea. This lady had never even intended to leave North Korea, but was captured and sex trafficked while on official business as a national swimming champion competing in China. She had come to faith once the man she was sold to had died and she was given refuge by Christians. She then made her way to Thailand where she was detained in prison. Through her witness, the Thai prison in which she was held was transformed and became a place of peace as more and more of the inmates found faith.

Biblical reflection

'So we are always of good courage. We know that while we are

at home in the body we are away from the Lord, for we walk by faith, not by sight.' (2 Corinthians 5:6-7 ESV)

Faith is the sphere in which we walk. And walking determines a movement forwards or journey in which we leave one place and arrive at another. So when we reflect on our North Korean family above, we cannot help but be challenged by the literal walk of faith that determined a new life, in a new country, potentially risking their own lives and the lives of those they left behind.

'Not by sight' does not describe the act of vision but emphasises the thing or shape not seen. This explains the phrase 'we are away from the Lord'. In this part of our lives, God is not physical or concrete, yet we walk in obedience and faith.

Reflecting on our own lives, when we walk by faith, how much more order and peace do we experience despite the circumstances around us? Faith is also a weapon of spiritual warfare, a defence against the work of evil.

'Above all, taking the shield of faith, wherewith ye shall be able to quench all the fiery darts of the wicked.' (Ephesians 6:16 KJV)

Faith cannot stand alone as a single tool of spiritual battle. It is part of a full set of defences included in Ephesians Chapter 6. Faith is accompanied by truth, righteousness, readiness for the gospel of peace, salvation and the Sword of the Spirit, which is the word of God as Paul writes. But faith is the largest weapon of defence as the shield held by each member of an army of believers whom Paul would have had in mind as he wrote this letter. Each shield interlocked with that of the next soldier, with the rear guard holding the shield above their heads to defend against the fiery darts of war.

What part do we play in this as we learn from our North

Korean brothers and sisters? Reading on from this verse, Paul declares the final strategy:

> *'And pray in the Spirit on all occasions with all kinds of prayers and requests. With this in mind, be alert and always keep on praying for all the Lord's people.'* (Ephesians 6:18)

Meeting North Korean defectors fuelled my faith. The oldest lady present told of her journeys back to the border to reach others with the good news, at the age of 86. She was so alive in her faith in Christ that she risks all for the gospel. She knows that, if she's caught by the authorities, she will be sent back to North Korea despite her South Korean citizenship. That's walking by faith!

Can we trust the same Father as we walk by faith through all this world throws at us and hold up our shield of faith, extinguishing the burning arrows as we go?

For it is not the size of our faith, but the authentic God in whom we have faith, who will bring us through whatever we face in the world.

Response and action

'Not all of us can go to Syria, Nigeria, Iraq or the many other countries around the world to help practically. But one thing all of us can do, and all of us must do, is pray.' That's what Paul Robinson, Release CEO, said in an encouragement to churches to join the International Day of Prayer for the persecuted church (IDOP). On IDOP Sunday in November each year, churches all over the world pray for their persecuted brothers and sisters, sharing their burdens in faith.

Will you and your church take up the fight in faith and stand with the global church in prayer for your persecuted brothers and sisters? Find out more and get the resources you need for

IDOP each year at www.releaseinternational.org

Chapter 7
Overcoming rejection – Pakistan and Laos

Creative input

Imagine a close friend has suffered a serious rejection: maybe their husband or wife has left them or they've been made redundant at work.

What would you say to comfort that person? Spend a few minutes writing down your response **before** reading any further.

Now imagine if you were the person who had been rejected. How would you feel about receiving the replies you have just given your friend? Would you be encouraged or discouraged?

Testimony

There are many positive characteristics we can learn about from members of Christ's worldwide church who are being persecuted: endurance, forgiveness, perseverance, grace, to name but a few. However, one area that we can often fail to consider is the issue of rejection, something very familiar to those who turn to Christ in Islamic, Buddhist and Hindu countries.

Many, if not all those I've had the privilege of meeting, have had to face, endure and overcome rejection to varying degrees. The greatest pain they carry is not a physical one but that of being cast out by those closest to them because of their coming to faith in Christ: teenagers abused and ostracised by their communities; young men beaten by their families; women humiliated or jailed. It is not surprising that those who decide to follow Jesus in hostile areas have had strong encounters with

God around the time of their conversions.

'Matthew' in Pakistan was locked up in a room by his family who threatened that they would kill him because of his choosing to follow Christ. God miraculously and literally opened a door for him to escape before they could carry out their threats. When a team from Release met him and talked about his experience with him, his sadness at being rejected by his own family members, siblings he had grown up with, was still very evident. This tender-hearted young man could only weep as we prayed for their salvation and his protection.

'Rose', another convert to Christianity, was asleep on the roof of her home when an intruder broke in and threw kerosene over her. As a result, she lost the baby she was carrying. She told us: 'I don't know the man who did this but I'm sure he was sent by my mother.'

It reminds us that Jesus said that he had not come to bring peace but a sword that would separate members of a family (Matthew 10:34). We too in the West can experience similar rejection: we may not be physically attacked or killed but we can still be rejected by family, work colleagues and others who think we've 'got religion'. We see similar scenarios played out across the world where individuals are seen to reject their native beliefs and choose what is perceived as a Western religion.

Those who come to faith in Christ in rural Laos, one of the few remaining communist countries and one of the poorest in East Asia, are likely to be rejected. Their family and village community may well believe that a conversion to Christ upsets the village spirits and so will mean something bad happening to their community as a result. The communist authorities, reminded of the attacks by the US on Laos during the Vietnam War, still suspect Western infiltration, while the majority Buddhists feel their religious identity is under threat.

'Grace', a young Laotian woman, was beaten, threatened with

prison and disowned by her family after coming to faith as a teenager. She told me: 'I felt very isolated at home and very lonely. And my dad would beat me and threaten me. My stepmother would curse at me.' Her father and stepmother even called the police to try to deter her from her new faith but Grace and six other girls who were also new believers refused to deny Christ.

How important it is therefore that as fellow members of Christ's family on earth we welcome and care for each other. To some degree we have all suffered rejection for our faith: maybe not to the same extent as Matthew, Rose or Grace, but most of us who have been Christians for a while have some understanding of what it is to be excluded or laughed at behind our backs or maybe to have faced discrimination or hostility.

Biblical reflection

Is blood really thicker than water?

In case you hadn't realised, members of your church are not perfect. But we need each other; we need to accept each other, and we need to focus on the eternal.

When Jesus said (in Matthew 19:29) that those who had left houses, family or farm because of him would receive a hundred times as much, he is referring to those who have sacrificed to follow him. Without a doubt, persecuted Christians fit into this category.

The saying 'blood is thicker than water' is usually employed to reinforce the idea that blood relations are more significant than other relationships, even if we don't get on with our blood relatives. However, the original meaning of this saying was quite the opposite: that those united by the 'blood of the covenant' are more important than those we are humanly related to through 'the water of the womb'. Those of us who are united by the blood shed by Christ and who have entered into God's covenant of acceptance and forgiveness are closer than our family relations. Those who have found that their relationship with Christ has led to division in their own family would understand the truth of this.

Conversely, we must be careful not to use our conversion to Christ as an excuse for intentionally or otherwise bringing division. It can be easy to cut off relationships with those we don't care for or find difficult by using the excuse that because they are not Christians we have nothing in common. We would be guilty of using our faith to reject others – something that sadly can occur when people embrace a new religion. One common characteristic of those converts to Christ rejected by their families is that they long to see their parents and siblings come to faith also, even if their love for Jesus has meant nothing but hatred and rejection from those closest to them.

How do we cope with rejection – our own and others?

So, how can we show acceptance to those who have been rejected? And if you've been rejected because of your faith, how can you know acceptance?

We can start by coming to the One who accepts all who come to him:

> '*Come to me,* ***all*** (my emphasis) *who are weary and burdened, and I will give you rest*' (Matthew 11:28).

Jesus was rejected by all, by the Jewish people he had come to serve and their religious leaders, the crowds, the Romans, even for a while by God his Father (crying out, '*My God, my God, why have you forsaken me?*') as he was left to die in the worst possible way (Matthew 27:46). Yet on that cross, what happens, what conversations take place? To John, Jesus says, '*Take care of your mother.*' To Mary, he says, '*Take care of your son*' (John 19:26-27).

In other words, 'accept each other into your lives'. He turns to the thief being crucified with him and declares:

'Today you will be with me in paradise' (Luke 23:43)

Both men have been rejected by society, but Jesus' final words are all about acceptance (for Mary, John and the thief).

If Jesus embodies acceptance, so must we to those around us, especially our brothers and sisters in Christ. Jesus was also pointing to the future: *'You* ***will be*** *with me in paradise'* (my emphasis). It is vital that we keep our focus on the future glory that God has in store for us rather than the present circumstances. As Paul writes in his first letter to the Corinthian church (1 Corinthians 2:9 NKJV):

'Eye has not seen, nor ear heard, nor have entered into the heart of man the things which God has prepared for those who love Him.'

It was, *'For the joy set before him he endured the cross'* (Hebrews 12:2).

In the same way, Matthew, Rose and Grace found love and support among the church, not just in words but in practical care. Rose now has a child of her own, Grace is married and serves in a church, and a Release partner cares for Matthew.

In a world that so easily finds excuses to reject people, let's give God's acceptance to those we meet, to show those desperate for true relationship that Jesus' arms - and the church's - are open wide.

Response and action

Are you struggling with feelings of rejection?

It can be hard to accept others today when we feel that we've been rejected ourselves in the past. As a counsellor friend often says: 'Hurt people hurt people.' Memories can surface and we feel the pain of rejection all over again. Sometimes it feels safest to pull down the shutters to protect our emotions and stop ourselves from being rejected again.

But what is God's response to rejection? Throughout the Old Testament the children of Israel repeatedly turn their back on God, chasing after false gods. The history of this rejection culminates in the rejection of God's own Son and his crucifixion. But, at that moment of complete rejection of Jesus, by the Jewish nation, the Gentiles and even for a period by the Father, the most profound act of acceptance is accomplished: through Jesus's rejection on the cross, we are accepted into relationship with God. Not just the Jewish race, but the whole of humanity, you and me.

So we need to remember that God accepts us in Christ and Jesus paid a high price for this to happen. No matter who rejects us – and as with those I've mentioned, it can be the people nearest to us – God accepts us. For some, accepting ourselves can be the hardest part.

Is the experience of your own rejection something that God can use to display acceptance to others? As you extend acceptance to others, ask him to heal your own memories of rejection.

How can I show acceptance to others?

Are there people in your life that you find difficult? (It's a silly question really.)

Are there people in your church or another part of your life who have been rejected?

Pray for an opportunity to help them to know that they are accepted by God and by you.

Reflect on this verse: '*Jesus is "the stone you builders rejected, which has become the cornerstone."*' (Acts 4:11). What is God saying about your own situation? Ask him to make something significant out of the rejection you have experienced.

Finally, pray for persecuted Christians, your true blood relatives, who have experienced rejection because of their faith in Jesus: people such as Matthew, Rose and Grace. One day you will meet them.

Chapter 8
Hope - Eritrea

'Behold, the eye of the Lord is on those who fear him, on those who hope in his steadfast love.' (Psalm 33:18 ESV)

'May the God of hope fill you with all joy and peace in believing, so that by the power of the Holy Spirit you may abound in hope.' (Romans 15:13 ESV)

Creative input

In Eritrean culture, the hope for coffee is a desire of many! This is not a quick occasion whereby you drop into a coffee shop, make your request and leave minutes later with a steaming cardboard cup, sipping it through a plastic lid. No, this is as much about community and the relationships formed around it.

Can you now make a strong coffee for yourself to smell? Fresh coffee will work better but instant is fine too. As you read over this description use your senses to be drawn into the life of an Eritrean. Read it slowly so you can give yourself a chance to 'feel' the story.

The coffee-making ceremony begins. Slowly gathering charcoal into a pile, fanning the glowing coals so that the flames diminish and the red and white colours of the heat radiate upwards out of the small tin burner. Feel the heat on your hand as you test its power. Then on to a flat skillet the coffee beans are poured and roasted. As they absorb the heat, a mellow but deep aroma drifts across your outside cooking area. This is your welcome. As neighbours and family begin to pick up that fragrance they begin to gather; to chat, to share news and to be. The beans are ready, skilfully crushed and poured into a traditional coffee pot, then brewed slowly over the coals. Intuitively you know when it's ready. You begin to pour the thick black coffee into small cups with plenty of sugar. You build the heat again, popping the corn to accompany the coffee. More people gather as the chattering increases over the coffee. Some laugh over stories whilst others share hopes and dreams.

In the refugee camps where so many Eritreans have escaped to, this ritual offers a continuity of culture, enables them to remember where they came from and hope for where they might end up. I witnessed this beautiful ritual in the dust of an Eritrean refugee camp in Ethiopia and I have seen it made on the linoleum floor of a woman's tiny flat in a European city where she had sought asylum after suffering imprisonment and persecution. Coffee - a picture of hope.

Testimony

Eritrea is perhaps one of the worst countries in the world for Christians to live in. President Isaias Afewerki has been in power since the country's independence in 1993. With no tolerated opposition and no elections since then, Afewerki's regime is built on a culture of perpetual fear fuelled by mass surveillance, intimidation, deprivation, compulsory long-term military service, arbitrary arrests, disappearances and killings. There was a general freedom to practise religion in Eritrea until 2002, when the government announced it would recognise only four religious communities: the Orthodox Church of Eritrea, Sunni Islam, the Roman Catholic Church and the Lutheran-affiliated Evangelical Church of Eritrea. Christians belonging to other denominations are not allowed to meet together for prayer, Bible study or worship. Since 2002, the government has jailed, tortured and killed numerous Eritreans for political and religious reasons, and thousands of Christians have been arrested and imprisoned. Prisoners, both men and women, are made to feel afraid, isolated and vulnerable, and made to believe that they can be disposed of by the state with impunity. They remain largely hidden from the world outside, stripped of their dignity and freedom. Several Christian prisoners have died in detention as a result of torture, the appalling conditions, or being refused medical treatment they needed. Those who die in prison are often buried unceremoniously by the guards, with their fellow inmates forced to dig the grave. Some prisoners have lost hope, surrendered to despair and committed suicide to escape the brutality.

John (pictured) is an Eritrean Christian who was imprisoned for seven-and-a-half years. In all that time, John never lost hope.

I first met John in Shire, a town in the Tigray region of northern Ethiopia, close to the refugee camp he was living in. John has an infectious sense of humour, a smile that lights up a room and, like most Eritreans, a love of good coffee. As he shared about his family, his childhood experiences, his friends, his imprisonment and his life in the refugee camp, he drew me into his world, his faith and his hopes and dreams for the future. John's world revolves around helping others, loving and serving God and caring for his wife and family.

I have been privileged to meet many Christians who have been imprisoned for their faith and I have met John on a number of occasions since. But I remember clearly the profound impact John had on me in that first meeting, as I listened to his words and I observed his character. Here I was listening to someone who had endured seven-and-a half years in a filthy prison in one of the harshest, hottest places on earth. Yet, all that I could see was this man's quiet confidence in God, a profound joy and love for life and for Jesus, someone who radiated Christ and who epitomized Romans 15:13 BSB – '*May the God of hope fill you with all joy and peace in believing, so that by the power of the Holy Spirit you may abound in hope.*'

John was full of hope; hope that was renewed by, and dependent upon, the promises of God. A hope that endured and was never lost, even in the darkest places and pain-filled experiences of his imprisonment.

When he started to tell me his story, I sensed that somehow this was going to help shape the ministry to prisoners of faith that I was engaged in. I also sensed it would change my understanding of how Release could best support Christians imprisoned because of their faith.

John continued to share with us but didn't dwell on the details of the beatings, the punishments, the conditions inside prison or the fears. He wouldn't be drawn into talking about his own experiences; rather, John wanted to talk about the other prisoners. He wanted to talk about his friend Mogos. As he shared there was no self-pitying, no questioning as to why God had allowed so many Christians to be imprisoned. For John, it was just the reality of being an evangelical Christian in Eritrea, a simple statement of fact, a God-given opportunity to live out his faith as a faithful follower of Jesus, regardless of the cost, an opportunity to serve and care for others.

I never actually had the privilege of meeting Mogos personally, because he died in prison in Assab, Eritrea. But thankfully God arranged that he would meet John, in Assab prison itself. Mogos wasn't a Christian when he was arrested and jailed, but this was the place where he found Christ. John shared the gospel with Mogos who then trusted Christ in a dark, dirty prison cell. The conditions in Assab are appalling, the heat unbearable, and the stench in the cells meant that guards rarely entered them.

Mogos had been suffering from intermittent vomiting and diarrhoea for twelve months when he was put in the same cell as John. He became so weak that John and another prisoner had to carry him to the toilet each morning. John faithfully washed and cared for his friend Mogos, but after just six months he was dead. John told me how he had led Mogos to faith in Christ, how he had taught him God's word, discipled him, fed him, cared for him, washed and treated his wounds and eventually buried him.

What he told me has stayed with me ever since. It made me cry out to God for answers to what had happened and why he had allowed it to happen. It also helped me to see how much John loved and valued his brother in Christ. It helped me to understand that God loved Mogos and had reached out to save him, giving him peace, joy and hope in the midst of incredible pain. I realised that God loved Mogos so much that he arranged for John to be not only in the same prison, but also in the same cell. God had a purpose for John being in prison and part of that purpose was to share the gospel with Mogos. God was wonderfully at work in this Eritrean prison. He was, and is, building his church, not just in Assab prison, but in prisons around the world in places such as North Korea, China and Iran where tens of thousands of Christians are imprisoned for their faith. Not only is God building his church in prisons, he is strengthening and refining that church. So many 'prisoners of faith' testify to having experienced God's presence, power and grace at specific times and in very tangible ways while they were incarcerated.

As John finished sharing his story, I asked him if there was anything we could do to help him, any way that Release might be a blessing to him. John's reply had a huge impact on me and underlined everything I had come to appreciate about my brother in Christ. He didn't ask anything for himself. He simply said that he hoped to be able to find Mogos's son. He had been told the son was living somewhere in Ethiopia and he hoped to share the same gospel with the son that he had shared with the father. He hoped he could tell Mogos's son how his father's life had been changed while in prison. He hoped that we might perhaps be willing to help him with his travel costs as he searched for the boy.

Release paid for John's travel to find Mogos's son. John was able to share the same gospel with the son that he had shared with his father. As I think about Mogos, I realise that all of his experience of knowing and loving Christ took place inside prison: his conversion, discipleship and death.

I reflect not just on John's words but also on his character, on the hope that I saw in John's smile and in his eyes. I understand that this was and is a 'living', deeply embedded, sustaining hope that doesn't guarantee easy answers but does assure us that all of God's promises are true. It's the assurance that nothing can or will separate us from the love of God in Christ – not even seven-and-a-half years in Assab prison.

Biblical reflection

Take a few moments to reflect quietly on the following verses in 1 Peter:

'Praise be to the God and Father of our Lord Jesus Christ! In his great mercy he has given us new birth into a living hope through the resurrection of Jesus Christ from the dead, and into an inheritance that can never perish, spoil or fade. This inheritance is kept in heaven for you, who through faith are shielded by God's power until the coming of the salvation that is ready to be revealed in the last time. In all this you greatly rejoice, though now for a little while you may have had to suffer grief in all kinds of trials. These have come so that the proven genuineness of your faith–of greater worth than gold, which perishes even though refined by fire–may result in praise, glory and honour when Jesus Christ is revealed. Though you have not seen him, you love him; and even though you do not see him now, you believe in him and are filled with an inexpressible and glorious joy, for you are receiving the end result of your faith, the salvation of your souls.' (1 Peter 1:3-9)

Even if your circumstances are incredibly difficult and you are not sure what to do, just acknowledge that God is your Father in heaven and that he will work all things together for the good of those who love him. (Romans 8:28)

If you are struggling, fearful or concerned, lift your head up and fix your eyes on Jesus and speak out the words of 1 Peter 1: 3-9. God will find a way and will renew his hope within you.

Photos of John on his release from Assab prison.

Response and action

Clench both fists as tight as you can, for as long as you can, until your knuckles go white. Feel the cramp and pain coming into the joints, the sharpness of your nails digging into the palms of your hands. Then slowly release your fingers and unravel the joints to flatten out your palms upwards.

Your hands have just experienced a tiny bit of the pain that John and Mogos would have felt being in such tiny spaces without water and fresh air, unable to move or correct their position to make it more comfortable. They would feel in greater agony as the blood returned to their feet or body as they were moved from one place to another.

Yet, we read that John did not dwell on this pain but instead focused on hope.

'In his great mercy he has given us new birth into a living hope through the resurrection of Jesus Christ from the dead, and into an inheritance that can never perish, spoil or fade.' (1 Peter 1:3-4)

Remember the coffee rituals where the scent gives people hope? Pray for Christians in Eritrea and those in refugee camps in Ethiopia as you smell coffee during your day. Whenever you have a hot drink, be it coffee or something else, remember them and the living hope within them.

Chapter 9
Overcoming - Nigeria

Creative input

The painting on the following page was inspired by the account of the Apostle Peter walking on water. I came across the painting not long after visiting Christians in Northern Nigeria who had been violently persecuted, and displaced many miles from their homes, by *Boko Haram*, a militant Islamist group which has caused havoc in Africa's most populous country.

Spend a few minutes just gazing at the painting, then read Matthew 14:22-33.

I wonder how many times Peter, as a fisherman, may have called out to God to rescue him from a storm. Well, during the storm you've just read about, with the wind beating down on him, Peter fixed his eyes and ears on Jesus, stepped out from the relative safety of the boat and walked through the swirling waves towards his Master.

Sometimes preachers focus on Peter 'sinking' but, let's be clear, Peter overcame fear and the very difficult circumstances of the storm, and walked through the waves! Before beginning to sink as the effects of the storm started to overwhelm him, Peter had initially overcome fear and the adversity of his immediate circumstances by putting his complete trust and confidence in Jesus and his word. And that hadn't stopped there. Once again as the adversity of his immediate circumstances caused Peter to temporarily lose sight of his Saviour he knew who to trust and called out to Jesus, who was of course there to 'immediately' save him.

'**Calling**' by Yongsung Kim, contemporary Korean artist.
Used with permission.

Jesus Walks on the Water

'Immediately Jesus made the disciples get into the boat and go on ahead of him to the other side, while he dismissed the crowd. After he had dismissed them, he went up on a mountainside by himself to pray. Later that night, he was there alone, and the boat was already a considerable distance from land, buffeted by the waves because the wind was against it. Shortly before dawn Jesus went out to them, walking on the lake. When the disciples saw him walking on the lake, they were terrified. "It's a ghost," they said, and cried out in fear. But Jesus immediately said to them: "Take courage! It is I. Don't be afraid." "Lord, if it's you," Peter replied, "tell me to come to you on the water." "Come," he said. Then Peter got down out of the boat, walked on the water and came toward Jesus. But when he saw the wind, he was afraid and, beginning to sink, cried out, "Lord, save me!" Immediately Jesus reached out his hand and caught him. "You of little faith," he said, "why did you doubt?" And when they climbed into the boat, the wind died down. Then those who were in the boat worshiped him, saying, "Truly you are the Son of God."'

Matthew 14:22-33.

On the pages that follow, you will read about Esta who faced the full force of *Boko Haram* and yet, rather than being overwhelmed, overcame!

After spending time with Esta, and other persecuted Christians around the world, I have come to realise that as they suffer the adversity of the most brutal of 'storms' they are not overwhelmed, as long they keep their eyes and ears fixed on Jesus. It has been remarkable for me to see how, trusting in Jesus, they so often experience the very best of God in the very worst of circumstances.

Hopefully, you and I will never have to face the adversity Esta faced, but we will certainly encounter many 'storms' and difficulties as we go through life. So, let us learn with our persecuted brothers and sisters that Jesus is ever-present to us through the Holy Spirit. Let us learn with them what it means to trust Jesus at all times so that, rather than being overwhelmed by the storms of life we will, with his help and by his grace, always be able to overcome adversity!

Testimony

At the start of 2015, Release International drafted a press release about north-east Nigeria. I was asked to read the press release before issuing it. I agreed its content and gave permission for it to be published. Then, I sat in my office, door closed, blinds down, and cried. Not just a few tears but many – the kind that feel as if they come from a place of torrent deep within. Here is part of that press release:

> 'Release International is again urging Nigeria to protect its vulnerable Christian minority in the north, following the latest massacre by *Boko Haram*.
>
> Female suicide bombers, said to be as young as ten, are the latest weapon to be used by terrorists in the

> wave of attacks in northern Nigeria.
>
> The latest attacks in Baga, Maiduguri and elsewhere, have forced 30,000 people to flee... An estimated 1.5m Nigerians have been displaced since the fighting began.
>
> The death toll from the insurgency has now reached 10,000...
>
> Many attacks have been against churches, schools and government buildings – especially in areas such as Maiduguri where Christians are in a sizeable minority. It's been estimated that *Boko Haram* have destroyed 1,000 churches since the start of their insurgency in 2009.'

I knew why I was crying: I was in danger of being overcome. The compassion I felt for the people represented by the statistics I'd just read pressed so heavily upon me that I felt as if I was being emotionally crushed.

At Release, we often talk about avoiding the use of statistics: numbers in isolation can 'de-personalise' suffering. Therefore, if we use them, we are careful to remember that every single number refers to a specific individual: a unique flesh-and-blood member of our Christian family, our brother, our sister!

The experience of one of my colleagues at Release illustrated this to me very well after he returned from Nigeria in 2014. He had spent time with many people and, as he described their suffering to me, his voice began to tremble. Barely holding back the tears, he said, 'Paul, they are no longer statistics to me: they are individual people; my brother, my sister.'

I share with you now the testimony of one of those dear sisters. Esta is a woman I spent time with in a camp Release has helped establish for internally displaced persons (IDPs) in northern Nigeria.

Touring the IDP camp with its director, I listened carefully to how so many men, women and children have had to abandon their homes and villages, repeatedly forced to flee from one place to another under the threat of *Boko Haram* violence.

Esta's village near to Gwoza had already been attacked by a small group of *Boko Haram* fighters, but the men of the village managed to chase them away. Then they came back, in larger numbers. It was seven o'clock in the evening and Esta's husband, Johanna, knew they had to leave. They ran for their lives, with bullets from automatic weapons spraying above their heads.

Having led his family away from immediate danger, Johanna, with one of their sons, returned to help others. A little while later, Esta heard screaming and she recognised it to be the voice of their son. Though still terrified, she and the other children ran back to where the screaming was coming from. Right there, they found Johanna dead, not far from their pastor's home which Johanna had obviously been trying to protect. Before killing him, *Boko Haram* fighters cut off Johanna's ears - and forced his son to watch.

In the middle of trauma and acute grief, it was left to Johanna's family to carry his corpse away to be buried. They dug a shallow grave and left Johanna there. They buried him next to another hastily dug, new grave.

That night, Esta was so traumatised she felt paralysed, 'like in a coma'. So she and her children, still in fear for their lives, waited in the bush until they could decide what to do.

As daylight came, they fled the area to see if they might find a place of safety. As their journey began, they passed their home and saw it had been burned down and their cattle killed. Moving on and passing Johanna's grave, they saw the one next to his had been opened and the corpse left in the sun. Their only consolation was that Johanna's body had been left alone.

Esta and her children spent three days trekking until they

arrived at Madagali. They were helped by people there but, three weeks later, *Boko Haram* attacked Madagali. They fled on foot to Michika.

In Michika, Esta and her children found some respite. Local Christians gathered food for them and even gave Esta a parcel of land to cultivate. But that respite was short-lived. One day, *Boko Haram* attacked the church Esta and others were meeting in. Esta escaped with two of her children and fled on to Mubi. Even now Esta does not know what happened to her other children: she has heard rumours that they are alive.

After five days in Mubi, *Boko Haram* attacked again so Esta and the children trekked for nine days to Lassa. As a consequence of that journey, Esta's whole body was so swollen that a man who helped them travel on to Yola thought she was pregnant.

They spent a month in Yola, where Release's partner rescued them, taking them to the relative safety of the IDP camp.

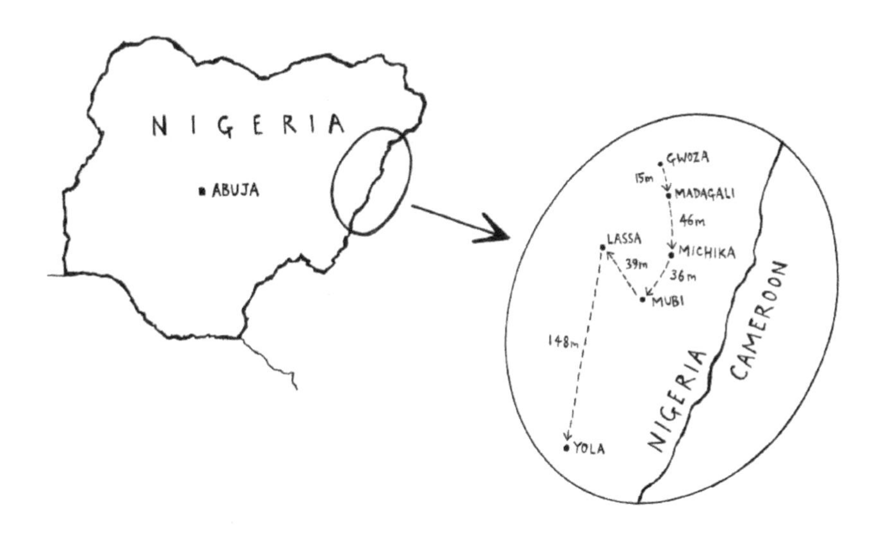

Map of Esta and her children's trek

Esta asked me to tell her story so that others will know what is happening in northern Nigeria, so that she and thousands like her might not be forgotten and abandoned (see Hebrews 13:3).

I have since had the privilege of visiting Esta again. What did I find? Was she living in despair or discouragement? Was she full of complaint, unforgiveness, bitterness or resentment? Given her journey so far, she has every reason to be. But no! She has, and continues to, overcome.

Even now, Esta is not living entirely free from threat. The IDP camp, though as secure as our partner can feasibly make it, is in an area where *Boko Haram* and Fulani militants have been active recently. The camp itself is no palace; far from it. Families live in spaces no more than three metres square. It is often very hot and noisy, and living in such a crowded environment is demanding. However, everyone I spoke with expressed gratitude for having a relatively safe place to live and recover. Particularly, those with children expressed their thanks because Release donors have made it possible for their young ones to receive ongoing education and medical care.

In further, conversation with Esta, I learnt that her health had deteriorated as a result of her terrifying ordeal and she now has heart problems and hypertension. She continues to have nightmares. And yet, she is grateful and joyful! Because her experience is all too common, she feels grateful to God that she is alive, knowing so many, including children, have been burned alive, killed with machetes or shot dead.

When I was with Esta this time, I watched as she led groups of internally displaced children in singing and dancing, helping them to worship the Lord and keep their 'home' culture alive. When Esta smiles, her face lights up as if the light and love of Jesus are piercing the darkness.

How can this be? How can anyone who has been through so much, be joyful or grateful, able to worship the Lord freely, enabling others to do the same?

Is it because Esta and others like her have faith in the living Lord Jesus, the Son of God? Sounds like a silly thing to ask, doesn't it? But it is a good question: after all, having faith, believing Jesus is the Son of God, is fundamental to overcoming the world.

Biblical reflection

'For everyone born of God overcomes the world.
This is the victory that has overcome the world, even our faith.
Who is it that overcomes the world? Only the one who believes
that Jesus is the Son of God.' (1 John 5:4-5)

It is said that John's use of the words, 'the world', refers to people and worldly systems hostile to the cause of Christ. It's worth noting that Jesus referred to Satan as '*the ruler of this world*' (John 12:31 ESV), and Paul said that he is '*the god of this world*' (2 Corinthians 4:4 ESV). So, when John talks about overcoming the world, he is talking about overcoming everything and everyone that stands in active rebellion against God and his Son Jesus Christ.

It's very tempting, when faced with trials, especially severe ones, to give up rather than to overcome. It's tempting, and a subtle work of the devil, to let the world and its ways creep in and overcome us. But that's not what we, as children of God, are called to. After all, it is an absolute truth that '*he who is in you is greater than he who is in the world*' (1 John 4:4 ESV). If that is true, and it is, how can the world overcome us?

Let's take that thinking a little further...

The night before Jesus was crucified, he prayed to his Father:

'I have given them your word, and the world has hated them
because they are not of the world, just as I am not of the world.

I do not ask that you take them out of the world,
but that you keep them from the evil one. They are not of the world,
just as I am not of the world. Sanctify them in the truth;
your word is truth. As you sent me into the world,
so I have sent them into the world.' (John 17:14-18 ESV)

I've heard Christians say, 'We are in the world but not of it.' It's a positive phrase but I believe that is the wrong order of things. Our starting point, as born-again believers in Christ, is not that we are in the world: our starting point is that we are already not of the world.

Author David Mathis, when considering this popular saying, seems to be thinking along the same lines:

'... Might this punchy phrase be giving the wrong impression about our (co)mission in this world as Christians? The motto could seem to give the drift, We are in this world, alas, but what we really need to do is make sure that we're not of it. In this way of configuring things, the starting place is our unfortunate condition of being "in" this world. Sigh. And our mission, it appears, is to not be "of" it. So the force is moving away from the world. "Rats, we're frustratingly stuck in this ole world, but let's marshal our best energies to not be of it.'[1]

Jesus does pray to the Father, asking him to keep his followers 'from the evil one', but we are not to live in the world with a defensive mentality, fearful in case we might be overcome by it. No, we are already not of the world, citizens of another kingdom (Philippians 3:20). We are in the world, yes, but on mission, sent into it with faith to overcome it!

[1]David Mathis is executive editor of desiringGod.org. Quote from his article: 'Let's revise the popular phrase "in, but not of"'

When I meet people such as Esta, I do not encounter those who are being overcome by the world, but people who are overcoming it by faith.

Yes, of course I do meet brothers and sisters who seem to be being overwhelmed by the terror and violence, but the grace of God can be found there too; the story for them is not yet over (cf. Philippians 1:6). How many of those, if found to be believing in Christ, will and do overcome?

The 'world' throws all kinds of things at us to distract us from developing an overcoming faith in Christ. Very often, we can be sucked into a 'Western' worldview that overcoming is about 'success': the accumulation of possessions, the size of our pay packets, job titles, the clothes we wear, or any of the myriad other status symbols that people cling to in our culture. But that's not overcoming the world, is it?

If we see those 'trinkets' of the world as signs of success or of overcoming, then it is likely that those are the very things in which we are placing our faith! And if our faith is in those things and not completely in Christ, when trial or hardship come our way, when we share in the sufferings of Christ, when the money dries up, or we lose our jobs, is there any wonder that our 'faith' seems to fall apart, leaving us in danger of being overcome by the world instead of overcoming it!

A friend of mine, who was a prisoner of faith in Eritrea, said to me recently, 'You know, Paul, I sometimes yearn for the prison cell. Safe here in the UK, I have it all: a nice car, house and ministry. It looks like I have "made it", at least to some degree. But these things draw me away from Christ and dull my faith. In the prison cell, all I had, everything I had, was him!'

Response and action

When I am with Christians who have been persecuted, I observe that those who have overcome terrible things and yet continue to praise God, have uncompromising belief in Christ. Not belief that is merely an intellectual recognition that he may have existed but, by the grace of God, a solid and secure conviction of the heart that he is the Son of God, that he is alive and is therefore '*able to do far more abundantly than all that we ask or think, according to the power at work within us*' (Ephesians 3:20 ESV).

They seem to be of those who can say, 'I don't just know "about" God, I "know" him' (cf. 2 Timothy 1:12). They have faith, as Shadrach, Meshach and Abednego did (Daniel 3), that confidently and steadfastly trusts God whatever the outcome might be. They trust in him alone. They believe, and know, he is with them, right in the centre of their suffering. In the midst of terror and violence, they cling to him like glue! Some, like Shadrach, Meshach and Abednego do not allow their faith to be compromised, even when threatened with death.

That kind of faith is always a challenge to me personally. Often, when I'm with people like that overseas, and always after I return, I spend time allowing their experiences and examples of discipleship to shine a light on my own. I spend time thinking about how well they are living for Jesus in the worst of situations. I look at my own life and contemplate ways in which I am called, each day, to overcome the world by faith.

If you are willing, that's the response I encourage you to make now. You will almost certainly not be facing death today on account of your faith in Christ. Your church will not be ransacked or burned to the ground on Sunday, with you in it. It's unlikely someone will harm you physically for speaking about the good news of the gospel of Christ. If you have children, it's not likely they are going to be attacked on the way home from school for believing in Jesus. However, it is highly likely this week, even today, that something will come your way that will give you opportunity to either compromise or to stand in Christ, overcoming the world by faith.

So spend some regular time prayerfully counting the cost of living more fully for Jesus in the midst of your own circumstances. Think about where you are placing your faith. Is it truly in Jesus or in the things of this world? Consider what you might face this week which will give you opportunities to overcome the world as an ambassador for Christ (2 Corinthians 5:18-21). Count the cost of doing so; think about some of the possible consequences and pray, so that, when those situations arise, you'll be ready to overcome by steadfast faith.

When Shadrach, Meshach and Abednego took their faithful and courageous stand before Nebuchadnezzar, they had no certainty that God would save them. They had no special knowledge or assurance they would survive the flames. They faced death and stood in faith anyway! Hopefully, for most of us today and this week, the things we face will not be quite so dramatic and costly. Even so, will we be able to say, like those three young men: Whether God rescues me or not, I will stand for him. I will not compromise my faith, and I will not deny my Lord. After all, that's the kind of faith which overcomes the world!

We hope you have been inspired by reading this book and engaging with the activities. If you would like to find out more about how Christians are undergoing, and responding to, persecution around the world or would like to feed back on how *Daring Devotion* has had an impact on you please call 01689 823491, email info@releaseinternational.org or visit our website www.releaseinternational.org We'd love to hear from you.

RELEASE INTERNATIONAL

Our vision is to see a world in which the whole Body of Christ understands persecution and responds prayerfully, pastorally and practically every time a Christian is persecuted.

We hope that you have enjoyed this devotional.

If you would like to read more about Christian persecution we recommend:

Tortured For Christ – written by Richard Wurmbrand, the Romanian pastor who inspired the founding of Release in 1968. Pastor Wurmbrand wrote this book after being imprisoned for a total of 14 years by the Romanian authorities in the 1950s and 1960s. The book is a classic story of Christian faith and endurance under extreme pressure and still has great relevance for today.

Throughout his time in prison Pastor Wurmbrand was tortured and brainwashed, yet he developed and maintained a Christ-like attitude of love and forgiveness towards his tormentors. The book is his inspiring story, his reflections on the persecution of Christians and his call to the Church in the West to remember its persecuted brothers and sisters around the world who even today are suffering for the sake of Jesus Christ.

We also recommend ***Jars of Clay*** which was written by Kenneth Harrod, a Release International member of staff who is an ordained minister and a former journalist.

Jars of Clay reminds us that persecution is at the centre of our Christian faith. The book gives a clear biblical perspective on persecution, and includes details of some of the persecuted believers from around the world whom the author has met as part of his ministry with Release. The book focuses on five key areas: mission, the gospel, grace, the church and hope. Each chapter concludes with a number of questions for personal reflection or discussion, making it ideal for use in a Bible study or home group or as the basis for a teaching series within your church.

Both books are available from:

Release International

Tel: 01689 823491

Email: info@releaseinternational.org or visit our website at: www.releaseinternational.org